An Italian Morning

Poems

Vinni Marie D'Ambrosio

Waterside Press, Inc.

Published in the United States
by Waterside Press, Inc., PO Box 1298, New York, NY 10009.

For more information, please visit the author's website at
www.vinnimarie.com

Library of Congress Cataloging–in–Publication data is pending.
ISBN 978–0–9615300–1–3

D'Ambrosio, Vinni Marie 1928–
  An italian morning : poems / Vinni Marie D'Ambrosio
  p 160 18 c. x 18 c. hardcover & softcover.

Graphic Designer: Cynthia F. Johnson, Rowayton, CT.
Printer: Blurb.com; Font is Goudy Old Style.

First Printing

Books, Poetry

Life of Touching Mouths
            (New York University Press)

Mexican Gothic
            (Blue Heron Press)

Book, Literary Criticism

Eliot Possessed: T.S. Eliot and FitzGerald's Rubáiyát
            (New York University Press)

Acknowledgments

ABAC (Bangkok, Thailand); Bitterroot; Brooklyn Literary Review; Confrontation; Cutbank; Glyph; Home Planet News; Inchcape Bell; Light; Loisaida; McGraw-Hill Book of Poetry; New York Times; Pagine (Rome, Italy); Pivot; Rattapallax; VIA: Voices in Italian Americana; Women's Coalition Journal.

for my beloved grandson
St. John Johnson

"Out at sea the dawn wind
Wrinkles and slides. I am here
Or there, or elsewhere. In my beginning."

Four Quartets, "East Coker"
T. S. Eliot

". . . quarried long ago in the haze
of an Italian morning . . . ."

An Italian Morning, "The Consolation in Being History"
Vinni Marie D'Ambrosio

Contents

II.   Helpings from a Chinese Restaurant

III.   Now, the Summer Trees

Paintings by Suzanne Gilliard

I. Amor Mundi

An Italian Morning

The Godspeed

On All Souls' Day, a visit to the family grave

Day of the Dead. An ordinary
gathering of generations
as though it were Sunday
at the grandfather's house.
The long parlor. The crowd
of faces stiffly floating
on the marble sea of
the mantelpiece. Under a shawl
of shadows, the piano.
And there, in a bowl
emitting almond perfume,
the sculpted marzipans.

The grandfather had earlier taken
a few of the painted fruits
to the cemetery
and in a sharp wind
made love's covenant
of apricots and peaches
with his wife, dead in 1924,
his small boy, in 1916,
his daughters, in 1921, '22, '23 —
on their headstone

carved above the tumble
of gray lilies and numerals,
a woman's frozen gaze.

At home, for his favorite
granddaughter,
the eldest, an undivined gift
waits in the dining room.
The idea, gracing
his narrow house for days,
came from an American movie
in which Loretta Young leaned forward
from the wall's glitter
into the world's real darkness,

tentative,
hands toward the audience,
and seemed to resemble
his grown son's grown girl.
Her asking look — *come una santa* —
unfurled his generosity
like the black parasols of memory
that sheltered maidens
from sun or rain.

The co-star — *un bel ragazzo* —
offered her a cigarette,
and spun out sweet promises
in a della Robbian wreathe
of smoke.

In the morning,
the grandfather had laid out
the gift,
first on the tablecloth,
then in the center
of the granddaughter's empty plate —
a tasty, smoky, beautiful
pack of Old Golds —
as the sign he approved her modern
habit and that her modesty
was inviolable,
as an example to teach
the gentleness of family
and the contentment
mercy makes possible,
and as his concession to her —
she is just nineteen.

Her cousins brush by
the great table,
hypnotized by the grandfather's
reversal.

On the dish,
in the shaft of cold light
entering from the backyard,
the cellophane wrapping is
a little bonfire.

But the granddaughter
(yet unblessed by
his Godspeed)
stands at the front parlor window
gazing at prophecy.
The gray air whitens,
curls, beckons — as wings upon wings
join in a November flight.

Amor Mundi

When? oh when will
    waiting hills
    hatch a drumbeat

    and the green
    strings of trees
    twang untouched

    and populations
    roam the valleys
    trombones at their lips

    grace notes
    unfurling
    morning glories

        Oh when? will
            brazen instruments
            chime

tunes
in the clarity
of fiery vines

and women and babies
dance with arpeggios
Are those *words*

those cadenzas
alive yet
only in heaven

And when? oh when will
our brute arrows
become burbling flutes

or tambourines
and sympathy be
at last unchained

and all the continents
uncontained

("Amor Mundi": Latin, "love of the world")

The Sensualist Buys a Pear

for Alex

The fruit vendor
huddles by his cart

bundled up in blankets
like a lumpy pear.

He's clapping red mittens —
and two apples dance

in the ice-spangled air.
Naturally I opt for Eve's apple!

And you choose with a whisper —
Rosy gold beauty! rubbing

a big pear on your coat's
foamy snow.   Soon *Succulent!*

and elated by the pear's truth
Perfect!   At last

casting its black seeds
past the vendor

mythic in the sucking
wind *I'll elevate that pear*

to mark our day! A monument. . . !
(We — young — our futures so long!)

Later ungloved
and warming we pore over books

in scattered piles
around your room

and are caught
by a tumble of planes

in a Braque still-life —
red apples and gold pears

flat yet oddly wild.
And in the stretch of evening

that looms ahead of us we
can't or won't decline

into the serious
or studious —

being wholly still–alive
with orchard light.

Samovar

for Alex, again

What comforts can I discern
under a snow-shattered twilight
(scarf, gloves, even my eyelashes

adorned by small pearls as though
I'm a beloved out of the steppes)?
Shying at broken rules and

breaking one. Crossing his threshold
deep into the hilarious bookish
dusty disorder of his room.

To sip tea spun Russian style
hot from a faucet into squat
glasses. To talk of

poems and poets — this, ages ago
in the fastness of his college dorm
in Cambridge, Massachusetts —

and he shutting the door.
But before the forbidden
lock can click

(and before
the sofa can confuse
our ceremonial selves)

from his samovar, that
in the old days of pogroms
ancestors had swaddled

in rags and hidden, here
set as serene as
a great and glossy yellow plum —

from his samovar, a gleam
of joy launches past the jamb
into conundrum's shadows.

Tenants in a Brooklyn Winter
   for R. H.

I'm blessed with a pair
of loving gay tenants.

One descends from English lords —
receives a salary, a pittance, for handling
Ticketron tickets to hit shows.
His mother and father
pay tithes in a California cult.
These are paradoxes hard to take.

From an upper floor this morning
he rang me around dawn:
"We have no heat."
Their north rooms
can be so bitter in winter —
and he, the world's
medieval dream of *courtesie!*
Quickly I toed the proper line and
phoned the sleeping
plumber's answering machine.

Next, I was going over bills —
still early — when
I looked up and he appeared
in the ice on my window's blur.
He was unlatching the frozen front gate,
stepping onto the walk,
tall and no hat,
then crossing over stiff blue snow —

past car-chaos on the parking lot,
past the pale two-story mural
of grapes and bananas and plums,
striding toward Abdul's Luncheonette,
out to buy a sandwich for the job,
and vanishing into the shop's disorder.

He never mentions it — but
his partner's been feeling poorly.

Someone,
give them a cornucopia.

Interlude: Three Unexpected Found-Poems Taken from Shakespeare's Plays

1. Prisoner of War

With scoffs and scorns and contumelious taunts
In open market place produced they me
To be a public spectacle to all.
'Here,' said they, 'is the terror of the French,
The scarecrow that affrights our children so.'
Then broke I from the officers that led me
And with my nails digged stones out of the ground
To hurl at the beholders of my shame.
My grisly countenance made others fly;
None durst come near for fear of sudden death.
In iron walls they deemed me not secure;
So great fear of my name 'mongst them were
    spread
That they supposed I could rend bars of steel
And spurn in pieces bars of adamant.
Wherefore a guard of chosen shot I had
That walked about me every minute while;

And if I did but stir out of my bed,
Ready were they to shoot me to the heart.

King Henry VI, Part One, I, iv.

2. Nervous Visitor

They say this town is full of cozenage:
As, nimble jugglers that deceive the eye,
Dark-working sorcerers that change the mind,
Soul-killing witches that deform the body,
Disguised cheaters, prating mountebanks,
And many such-like liberties of sin:
If it proves so, I will be gone the sooner.

Comedy of Errors, I, ii.

3. Go and Write Her a Love Poem

Say that upon the altar of her beauty
You sacrifice your tears, your sighs, your heart.
Write till your ink be dry, and with your tears

Moist it again, and frame some feeling line
That may discover such integrity.

For Orpheus' lute was strung with poets' sinews,
Whose golden touch could soften steel and stones,
Make tigers tame, and huge leviathans

Forsake unsounded deeps to dance on sands.

Two Gentlemen of Verona, III, ii.

Gravity in Mexico

for Ramón

Roaming like moons
inside a ring of hills
we smiled all day

wore the wind as earrings
let it roll diamonds
up and down our fingers.

All day the wind was wheels
churning our bodies.

Breeze bands
careened around us.

One eely loop of wind
bumped an iguana
caromed up
landed high in a yucca and spun
into twins!

But the hills were grave.
Light lay there
like smooth fruit

weighing yellow in the afternoon
then red and heavy in the evening.

The Painter Yearning for Her Lake

for Suzanne Gilliard

Daffodils
grow from her fingernails.
A handshake — and they languish!

This is no slight
slough she's in,
because she's generous,

and phlox and orchids shoot
from her eyes,
and the city's sights
don't suit them.

If only we could halt the truckers
and pedestrians, or
pluck some salesmen
out from the shadows, she'd
haunt them,
in a sylvan way.

Here, she serves all elixirs —
a yeoman, busy,
stretching her green scenes —

and she breathes flux
into our labor.

Poets, when next we
open shop blinds
and catch dawn flashing
on the concrete walks,

I'll bet you a sestina that
our susurrous work-pots
will be swirling with her
dampening orchids' and
daffodils' petals, her

wild gardens staining
the vortex of our spreading poems.

Love Upstate

I.   Poems,
      memory,
      and love
      are meter, not matter.

      Reader, don't
      for a moment
      think
      they are flesh.

II.   You see,
      I'm not in San Francisco, not
      disorganizing a plate
      of antipasto
      in a shady garden restaurant,
      not facing a kindly gaze,
      but their shapes
      draw me like the wind.

III.   Here's a stanza tracing a shape,
             a horseshoe. Long ago, a tall Cavaliere
       meets a girl — my mother's being
  is being begun! For good luck, check
out the horse/shoe
of her Papa's stallion.
          See its twin prongs throbbing
              spondees and forked lightning.
                    Iron is absent, and hardly missed.

IV. This stanza cradles a foetal curve —
       above a beach, a halfmoon rocking
          the pair who eloped my lifetime ago. . . .
        Look, the moon-beams varnish
          a tree while its black leaves turn
       jazzy and shimmy and shake.
     Half/moon, not really half-unborn.
    Well, didn't I lie there in sweet caul?
Was I on the dark part or luminescent?

V.   I'm not
incurious, or inattentive, or indifferent to
the thick places.
In a poem we drift straight through
    solidities, even
through this Brooklyn house
with its limestone façade
and long intricate curtains bracing
against the wind.

VI.   Once, flying
to the West Coast
in a high lonely plane
over a pearly jungle of clouds,
I saw in the sunshine
a great rain-ring,
a round spectrum
balancing in the sky,
a target
for a rapturous arrow.

VII.   This part of the poem
       is the memory of a marigold.

       Upstate, New York.

       We crouch, denims touching.

       Our faces dome it: we smell its
       yellow lineaments —
       odor of bookstores,
       nutmeg,
       sharp heat!

       A heliograph!

       A trumpet of topaz
       flourishing for a Shakespearean king
       lazing in the countryside.

       His hand in love with my hand:
       we take the marigold, and it
       umbrellas our morning.

We are special, as in a Renoir,
and the air is washing meadows.

He knows a blue lake beyond the hill.
The land is like cake just for me
Far into my memory a childish *chanson*
    winds out
of a park band. . . "*Vrai, vrai*. . .,"
and a carousel purrs, residence
of wooden horses festooned in gold,
ideal, their moulds
ascending along red poles, spool-turned,
turning,
and ascending.

And we, ascended to the hill's lip,
touch the empty sky.
Below us
lies the dry and shining biscuit, the lake
unlaked,
its light stable and sunken,

a half–built causeway
gashing it.

I am yet dreaming that chasm blue.

And so we run zigzag down in love
to the gray bowl, the green and sensual
    hills circling it,
and we pluck two arid gray gifts,
branches,
so desiccated as to seem solid dust,
in the shape of birds flying,
tense,

when one hill strikes a chord,

marvelous concussion,
and strange!
a paper comb and mixmasters
and Moussorgsky at once,
and I startle the way a deer does,
mute,

my neck lengthened, and he cocks his
    head,

and soon the hill spins out a thick tuning
    arc
of birds,
a long low rainbow in shuddering blacks
    and silvers
that hums,
and brakes, and we rise
to stop the disappearance of the huge
    smooth song
over the other lip of the earth,

but we are left with two dry drowned forms
in our passionate hands.

Maine Chance

1. **Summer, pianissimo**
Mary speaks

I moved to Maine
with my pen ready
and a greed for beauty —
the silence that swung

from pine to pine
giddied me —
days — *pianissimo* —
bee-lined through summer —

I had lusty swims —
shaggy green hikes —
no — they had me —
while my poems rode

round and round
in the various air —
soon the days of winter —
my windows how

bewitching
in their booming glory —
red skies calling me
to the frozen sills —

but then
summer's amity! —
the embraces of blue coves

and soft springing trails —

once more
bird-tweets in mute trees —
always and again
beauty remaining unpenned —

wild —
riding every

puff of wind
and thundersquall

2. **Winter, fortissimo**

Mary's friend speaks

what would you do
for dear Mary who cries out on the telephone
each winter
"How many sunsets can one watch!" —
whose heart stands still when
the livid skies burn
orange and gold flames
at her windows — the beauty
estranging — seeming to roar like
the city she fled, with its same din? —

    and then no words staying to tell
    what she had wanted her poetry to tell —

    of silence in a nave —
    the lidded nuns — the lights
    in crimson tumblers
    tap-dancing for her mama
    laid out on pleated satin —

    or from a deeper past —

of ancestral Celts
crackling torches and black woe
in Etruscan valleys —

by the frozen sill
she stares at the sky's red glory —
enchanted — paralyzed —

disgraced —
while flecks of poems fall
behind the hills that face her —

and her pining winter journal
lies closed on the table —

and Maine's solid ice
blushes —
then darkens —

Grand Tour

He murmured,
Love with you is seeing a
fiery sunrise on the
blue,
blue,
blue
Mediterranean.
She was breathing the shallows among dark
planets,
but thought I'll join him
in scenery-gazing.
So she floated to Europe.
And there beyond the bathing shore,
there along combustion's blue edge,
there curried by the orient light,
a ship slid
like a slow pearl swan,
and she loved it to swooning,
and again lost his sky and his sea.

The Blue-Ringed Tower in
El Centro, CA

for Linda Lopez McAlister

I left for El Centro
in the month of January, when
the gulls were chunking eels

in Sheepshead Bay.

The first hours in the deep
Imperial Valley stood brilliant
on corundum, emery, quartz.

I awoke the second day
to an adobe garden, was enchanted
by wrought-iron and roses

and the smooth trunk
of a palo verde.   Soon
a hummingbird struck
the lush midair near a vine,
and with a yellow whirr scraped the space,

chopped out a niche,
flailed it wide enough
to vacuum-pack a small wooden saint

or (a later thought
      when love had somewhat
      shrunken me)
to be filled with the half-million poor
in nearby Mexicali
who were pinched dry by chollas
and might be held for an instant
in the hummingbird's hollow
as a nest-egg for a poem.

    I.
    On my daily drive to Calexico,
    I passed a broad tower
    a hundred feet high,
    banded near the top
    with a blue painted ribbon.

The lower desert was drawing me,
but I resisted the dry immersion.

II.
The turquoise–ringed tower
on one sleepy trip
became the knuckle
of a Mexican cacique
exiled in anger nine
foreign miles from home.

I gorged on the neighborhood's *carne asada*
cooked over fire on fiery afternoons
in the tough shapes of iguana,
and I licked at beer
salty as the mineral world.

III.
The tower then was a bride's thumb,
dreamily belted by dust and blue satin.

In the season when tons of carrots
were hauled from the Valley, and the sky
very dark, cattle feedlots silent,
I fought a minor earthquake,
noting at dawn
the long watery gleams

on the patio
at the pool's narrow end.

IV.
Whoever was it told me —
sotto voce —
that the tower was a cauldron,
that it burned elements
to remake deserts?
I saw a startling power
(speeding home one night)
when its blue–bricked fist
stretched towards a comet.

Wearing thick sneakers
(advised by postcards in arcaded shops)
I went down into the desert
the week it was "a carpet of bloom."
Although two or three nettles
pierced rubber and skin,
among whispered hisses
I hopped and pulled them out,
and my first gray coyote

flashed over the carpet of bloom
like the shadow of a moment's tree.

      V.
      As for the tower, it wasn't a tower
      but a vat,
      the biggest in the Valley;
      through irrigant pipes it rained
      on the fields,
      and the owners of the nitrate plant
      had hung the bracelet on it.

At Easter break, in Mexicali,
a beggar sang *Canción Mixteca*,
blind, grazed thin by the half–million:
"¡Qué lejos estoy del suelo donde he nacido!"
("How far the place where I was born!")
I bought the blue song,
and some stone rings for my mother and sister,
and a multiflowered tin–framed mirror.

VI.
Then I learned, at last, that high in the air
the robin's–egg circle
had been painted precisely at sea level.

And on the daily drive
from El Centro to Calexico
that blue bangle was a miracle,
caught on a post that was nailed deep
as my Datsun in the Valley,
a sapphire hoop
waiting to sail
straight east or south or west,
through caves below the mountains,
till it came to a perfect
skim on open water, always,
now, touching the foam
and never scooping so much as a drop
of the Baja Bay or Mexican Gulf
or Mediterranean or Indian Seas,

faithful to its path,
a delicate performance.

Meditations on the Seven Deadly Sins

(i) pride (ii) gluttony (iii) avarice (iv) envy (v) wrath
  (vi) lust (vii) sloth

(i)
a triple play!
thousands of teeth glinting
at the team

(ii)
peaches nel vino
pasta! pomodori! formaggio!
o sole mio . . .

(iii)
on tip-toe
toward me — hordes of hyenas?
tax collectors?

(iv)
rosy trees arching
over mommas and prams
and an aching old woman

(v)
FINALLY
ELECTION DAY!
-!!@3**\<!#+!!

(vi)
lad caught
by the airy dance of
a lass — O!

(vii)
snores
in wintry darkness
the thinning bear

Love Has Pitched His Tent
in Two Dimensions

(in response to "Crazy Jane Talks with the Bishop"
by William Butler Yeats)

I met a man
on daisied shore,
he kissed my shoulder
and my thigh,

kissed me more
and more and more,
and then begged
to say goodbye.

O, from the blue
broke harpsichord,
sadly danced
the cumuli!

*   *   *

I penned a me-
dieval round,
a virelay
in sweet music

about our bathe
in goldfish pond
and honeyed hour
in darkling nook,

then schooling him with
my lilting sound,
I pressed him in
a Romance book!

*   *   *

Chivalry learnt —
now faithfully wan —
the ruing lover's
to foolscap gone.

An Italian Morning

II.   Helpings from a Chinese Restaurant

Trio, with Brass Solo

On trumpet he's elated
this warmish afternoon

trilling minor sevenths
quoting old riffs

even blowing Doomsday
while leaning on his shadow in the cellar

It's so jazzy!
He's "found a new Baby!
found a new girl!" O whatta bay-bay-Baby

   and his music   quickens   empty corners
     and zigzags   dusty   bellies of bottles
       curls through   the hill of junk

His wife? she's kneeling
in their garden and breathing
the dancing air, she's tumbling music
and bulbs under the earth, she's

dreaming that when summer
unfurls, his notes will come up

gaily printed on tiger lilies
He closes his eyes
blowing far out   miles out   to his new Baby

   cadences   up airy ladders   and toots
     and tongue-tipped   harmonies
       and satiny jumps. . .

Above the roof, wings of pigeons
rustle in counterpoint

and cloak Gabriel, that revelation
guy who's floating lazily in the blue on high
quiet and incorporeal

No cloud is yet flaming

   and the archangelic April sky   swings
     sweetly pliant
        O gardener   O Baby   soon
           too soon   too soon
             both bound   for crying

Helpings from a Chinese Restaurant

Confucian,
dainty —
having been scripted
in simple red print
by monks wrapped
in the papery mists
of Asia's mountains —
great Words for the Ages
leap from crispy tricorns.

Naturally
their dreaming authors
want me to take
such declarations to heart,
so I tape the wee slips
by the dozens to my desk,
where they flutter
and wrinkle
and age to gray.

Never will I cast them —
my hoard of prophecies
for a Perfect Life —
into that evil trash basket,

Unfulfillment,
standing by my knee
so ravenous!

> "Numerous pleasurable adventures
> are in store for you!"
> "Many new friends will be attracted
> to your charming ways!"
> "An inch of time
> is an inch of gold."

When I'm in my study
with those jolly confetti,

just call me fortunate.

Mosca the Cat Meets a Dragon

A snakey pile of leaves, like an old sleeping
      dragon, rusty, papery, snorting in its windy
      Manchurian dream, my cat boxing with
      its leafy toes,

explodes!
makes her backbone bowed!
then she's a sprung fur arrow hammering
at the Blankinships' flapping ailanthus

till high in the sun's sawdust
nailing her cat–hug
she acts the anonymous
Ionic capital.

At a bay window, the pane seamless,
I somehow bond with her,

she harbors so hard,

her eyes brass screws
in the wrinkling jungle,

all those stalks cross–hatching,
all those leaves
unhinging.

Aubade: The Spousal Parting

I see him
clearly

After years of
no song

my days are gorgeous
and long

I keep vigil over their
hints, how they're flourishing
into the frankest garden
of insistences

My days spring
miracled

Their horizons pulse, shift
like shelves
around him
and in a stroke of decorum

like a cloud a golden puff a god-feast
he is placed!

This worship itself a ballooning loaf yes it
glees me I

love it

and I swear to lay this *pain d'épice*
on the many altars
in tenements and governmental palaces

chanting a wish
for joy to burst
from the spigot
on his soul
daily

with urgent sunrise

Fragonard in the Rumble-Seat

Your skin,
the shunted clothing, my skin, the policeman's
flashing light, dim for twenty years.
Now they relume as icons
in your catalogue of dreamy
what-ifs. Drinking, you look beyond
my summer bronchitis, beyond
the Italian restaurant's plump banquette
of red vinyl unfolding and
returning as a rumble-seat below dark
and deep trees. Your interstate efficiencies,
wife in the Midwest, present urges — these fade
into your wistful "What if —

> that time — we had made it?"

At the lake,
the lake is a black conch
filled with the secrets of sunset.
Peaches and pinks have slipped inside,
the crest of privacy. Trilliums simplify,
and berries are absorbed by bushes.
Birds, sucked into balls, harbor the day's chords.
And yet a policeman, ravishing the

Dodge, suddenly
frames our parts in preclimax on a drumhead of
rococco light,
for you and him and me
to savor in surprise forever.

        Old friend, haven't we all "made it"
in our museums of loss?
You, picture–abductor,
holding the scene as ransom
in your mulish marriage. He, in heated labor
curating forgeries to bribe Death.
And I, lover of still–lifes,
gazing at this small mirror,
this compact glowing beside my brandy,
wondering, shall I escape the sheen
in breathlessness and obliterate
its lingering flash, skin, and skin?

Interlude: Three Found–Poems from Herman Melville's **Moby–Dick**

1. Mourners, at Entablatures for Men Lost at Sea

Oh! ye whose dead lie buried
beneath the green grass;

who standing among flowers
can say — here,
here lies my beloved;

ye know not
the desolation
that broods in bosoms like these.

What bitter blanks
in those black–bordered marbles
which cover no ashes!

What despair in those
immovable inscriptions!

What deadly voids
and unbidden infidel–
ities in the lines

that seem to gnaw
upon all Faith,

and refuse resurrections
to the beings who have
placelessly perished
without a grave.

As well might those tablets stand
in the cave
of Elephanta
as here.

2. Pulpit

Its panelled front
was in the likeness of
a ship's
bluff bow,

and the Holy Bible
rested
on a projecting
piece of scroll work,
fashioned after
a ship's
fiddle-headed beak.

What could be more full
of meaning?—
For the pulpit is ever this earth's
foremost part;

all the rest comes in its rear;
the pulpit
leads the world.

From thence it is
the storm

of God's quick wrath is
first descried,

and the bow must bear the earliest
brunt.

From thence it is
the God of breezes
fair or foul is
first invoked for favorable winds.

Yes, the world's a ship
on its passage out,
and not a voyage complete;

and the pulpit is
its prow.

3. Nuptials By-the-Sea

In New Bed-
ford,
fathers, they say, give
whales for
dowers to their daughters,
and por-
tion off their nieces
with a few por-
poises a-piece.

You must go to New Bed-
ford
to see
a brilliant wed-
ding; for,
they say, they
have reser-
voirs
of oil in every house,

and every
night recklessly
burn

their lengths in sperm–
aceti

candles.

Taking Tom to the Party

My cat died last week,
yet there she flies! — tricking
the corner of my eye,
scuttling imparadised out
to the hall — while the women

inside the room, not quite filled
with *Four Quartets,*
linger on for more Eliot and tea.

I whiz off, tacking
downtown — almost merry
in the eddies of an autumn wind
that carries my glimpse
of old Mosca —

and stop dead at
Union Square Park!

An odd calm there.
Beggars, clumped under trees,

eating hugely, silently —
thickets of merchants, feeding
against leafy walls —
children, flourishing forks,
their skateboards lizards in a doze.

This stillness,
this curry,
these hundred bowls of golden
    razzle-dazzle —
where from?

To the side, cast in bronze as if in a stride
level with the blind crowd,
it's the near-naked saint of the Ganga
hosting his own birthday party! —
bespectacled, smiling at the mysteries
of Manhattan's unyielding buildings.

And in a ring around him,
Eliot's dark red roses —
gnarly and spell-struck —
are moored to the air.

Mystery

I.

Why does he pray, every Sunday,
the old man in the pew before me —

"May my wife see the light" — ? Every Sunday,
during the parish

Intercessions, the same words float
in a cavernous whisper from his massive

chest. His head, even bowed, seems monumental,
its crop of whiteness

like a buffalo's mane in moonlight.
I hear him clearly — always he's chosen

the second row, and ritually I take the third.
And always

nearby he has the same black suitcase,
its canvas sides stuffed to bursting —

with what pantomime of possessions I
don't know.

Standing, we each hang onto
the warm wooden bench-backs,

red hymnal in hand, thin pages lying still.
No gilded transept

or carved mahogany baldachin faces us
but an altar that's plain as the plainsong

spiraling down in clear gray air from an invisible
grove of singers.

II.

I'm not certain I should be revealing all this —
that at the entreaties for Intercession

I've learned to anticipate the pained,
private words,

"May my wife see the light,"
rolling around soft and deep.

The incantation — is it his eleventh–hour
love, or

the warning crack of doom?   You can see how
a person might come to dwell

on this Byzantine triptych — an ancient and
homeless groom, a rusty

and hopeless bride (her gaze darkly averted,
his flaming), and, between the two,

a figure of mystery leaning one way and then
the other, listening.

Fadeout in Washington Square Park

He's not physically busy,
but his mind jives jazz.
Above him a lamppost
holds a jubilation

of five moons. He rehearses
his coiled music, he glistens
from wattage flowing
over him.

In the sunken hour
past, his analyst has conferred
life, and now he leans
against the fence's

sparkles, perceptions
drenching him, heel
on the iron crossbar.
He's in a Hollywood glossy,

allowing love to fade. . . .
And she comes, fading,
toward him from *her*
analyst, jelling the weekly

script — "Leave him!" —
lilting it. And stops.
Wingless, the two are caught
by the one thought,

and can't possibly take note
of the cat scurrying
into penumbral space
after a squirrel or a sparrow

or some other small
sorrow — or no sorrow
at all but a tree–blossom
lifting and dropping

through the hovering dusk.

The American Wouldsman

On noting that the "American Finance Association
will make a field trip to Chase Manhattan Bank."

What bonny bank,
what buffalo-haunted stream,
will you be chasing off to now?

Fawning, dappled
by efflorescent glints,
will you scent out mysteries
and turn into tellers
of antique tales?

In green-columned forest
will you check
your wrinkling dolors

and fold away your foxgloves
in a golden patch?

Or will you cut a sprig of rue
and, like your cheaping cousins,
will you bill and coup?

Oh breathe it, breathe it,
pecuniary pals,
the fragrance of the mint!

Lovers all,
roll, uncomptrolled,
in the clover!

Judgment Day at Luquillo Beach

breeze
blowing mightily

three seaworn chairs
overflowing with
poet and wife
flipping pages
of bestsellers
and my Romeo
his hot glances
on the move
a too-tight trio
I'd say really a single squid

my lonely chair
slapping at air

I tell you what —
go! double-quick
snatch a pineapple
from the vendor downwind
drowsing in his bower

and a stiletto to gouge
out its prickly eyes
and run
at the bending green sea

but the knife lies shy
in my hand
merely blinking silver points
onto the swells!

and my victim vaults double-quick —
drunk on redemption —
over whooshing meadows of foam
spiny tail a comet
in and out of clouds
reeling up
all the world's crimes
sending them
pinwheeling
into the sun's yellow blast!
*

now
wind tame
beach serene

Caribbean waters
twinkling blue

poet and wife napping
swaddled
in colors of tropical fish

Romeo caressing
his shoulders
with creams from Rome

well I stash
my dollar at last
with the pineapple vendor

who whispers to me
in tender puertorican

¡Vaya! my child
sin no more

On a Chow Walk

for my dear sister, Maxine

Featherweed,
a vast view of them
blowing in a warm wind.

Mark off a circle in a Brooklyn marsh,
a large one.
Don't come in. Watch us.

The sand is wet
and magic
is cocooned there.

Tiny crabs
sidling by,
rapidly.

An earthworm
easing out rubies,
silently.

My chow freshens his coat
on peripheral
clumps,

and I drag his protection-stick.

It's a pacific stick.
No enemies on
the weedline
that silvers the horizon.

But nine kids
spill from a weedcave
chattering as if
they've escaped from a witch.

It does not help
to know French
Italian
Spanish
when confronted with Armenian.

And there we are,
the houses brown and farhuddled,
the creeks crisscrossing
hexes beneath the feathers.

I don't say a word,
I draw an elephant in the sand.

They applaud me
by knocking elbows
knowingly.

With the protection-stick
I draw a very big
rhinoceros.

Their foreign tongues
click
paragraphs.

With my stick
I make the biggest tiger
you ever saw, its tail
twelve feet long,
the rubied earthworm
in its eye.

"Aahh!" they whisper
in Armenian,
in a lovely minor
key.

The marsh circle is
filled with beasts,
and we trudge around
stamping out the beasts.

Not sadly, you know.
We're all waiting
for my grandest
sandjob.

So I make a wavyhaired
woman
riding a horse,
and parading behind her

a cat, a dog, a duck,
a mouse, a parrot,
and with his fourth limb
kicking the weedrim,
a handspringing
monkey.

Some of the kids
turn a few handsprings.
One meows.
Two bark.

And above us,
gulls
crown the marsh.

If Cabbages Was Kings

I play the piano rotten
I sing rotten

I touch trees good
I wake up good

If only I was a piano-bird and the pear-tree's
           flowers my ivories!

If only the morning sun down in my yawn was
           mezzo-soprano!

III.   Now, the Summer Trees

Bungalow

It's nice to come home
to that green-shuttered bungalow
in the umbrella-tree-lined lane

I mean the
body
in its palpability

after having had a transcendental
fling

I mean

after I've flipped through
one of my Irrational Geographics
I have an amiable feeling

Though like any returned traveler
there sneaks a slight superiority
into my spirit vis-à-vis
that bungalow-body
Anyway

I'm back back
hi eye
howdy
body

Yes
the luggage was light

Now, the Summer Trees

I always had
a leafy view

— could linger by
my window sill,

palms cupped
for the vagrant dew —

at five,
at forty,

and now too.

Flight of the Imagination

He's still there, doesn't move
from the window enclosing my terrace.
A very big Fly.

On one black almond, two oval
glints of blue. Stretching
outward — six etched lines

kinked into wispy angles.
And wings, arrowheads
almost pink, pointing

this Fly to true East
on the glassy map that faces me.
If I tilt my head to the right —

and I do — the Fly, a hypnotic lump,
seems to float backward
West on a ripple

of gingko leaves. Tilt
more and, still in reverse,
the Fly skids across

a shiny pane on the face
of a brownstone — his private pond
edged with damask flowers!

Now leaning right from my rump,
I direct the Fly in a swoop
at the tall fellow who strolls the walk below —

a thinking man, his purple cap
clamped on tight — and our Fly's sitting
on the shoulder seam of his tie-dyed

shirt. Lord, this Fly's a backpack!
Riding to Hawaii !   I'm filled with power,
can aim him at anything,

he's an unmoving
movable, my slavey,
ready for a jaunt!

I bend my head left, and he swings
East, his wings opals
paralyzed in earth eons ago.

For the last touch, I crouch a half-inch.
This wad of summer sloth, still clinging
to the glass, smoothly

noses into clouds that streak the sky —
toward Granada and sherry and a flamenco
at dawn with a Spanish Fly!

A Cheerful Morning's Report

"Because I could not stop for Death –
He kindly stopped for me – " Emily Dickinson

We all feel awful
because the cat has cancer —
although today you wouldn't know it.

It's dawn.
She dogs Don's steps,
throws herself down
on the skiddy linoleum,
silver belly toward ceiling.
Hopes to be tickled,
but his each foot floats on.

She shadows more steps,
and throws herself down
on shiny plank floor
before her napping-chair,
silver belly a bellows,
purring now —
pleading — for a tickle.
And still he keeps to business.

She follows longer steps,
flings self in a roll
onto woolly rug,
claws all dependent,
belly ready. Hopeless!

Again then on pale tiles,
belly round,
a provocative hill, and —

as winter's air rushes in,
the New York Times held
high in one hand —

he answers her wooing
by scratching her coat
(oh my, is he her Old Scratch?)
and laughing,
"Now I've got you!"

Veronica

I knew it kept me rare to tell my
rare friends from Queens
we must avoid a bull
when we debarked the BMT.

Above the low platform, skies
raced in from New York City, but not
faster than that bull. I
advised us to hide

our red scarves or red gloves as
we left the open station, and stuff
them into school bags, and speed
cutting for my house, and duck

by the soft blank lots,
the black clouds collapsing in
folds on the horizons, building
us a breathing bullring.

It was true. A bull lived
in my Brooklyn then,
in Flatlands. A dark ton,
the core of the arena, beware —

he mashed the lots
riding on the Queen Anne's lace
straight for a ruby cross
or anything that was red. . . .

Those days we were in residence
in a brick two-story
mortared on the marshes, its
long stoop willful, its

cellar's eyes sinking, those
days when Wendell Wilkie and
then Tom Dewey were lost
embattled issues

in the solid brick house of
my father's governance, where,
slowly being crossed, my
father was — yes, baited —

executing his
own growing veronica.

Interlude: Six Translations from the Spanish of Poet Alfonsina Storni (Argentina, 1892–1938)

1. That's It

Sometimes my lines come
from the ideal.

At others, from storms of anguish
in my breast.

And at others, in some oracle's urge
to force words.

But so often, friends, they spring
from vanity.

I am, simply, a common mix
of goddess and beast.

2. Humility

I'm the one who paraded proud
With sham gold on her shoulders —
A few poems — and believed she was grand.
Her harvest gorgeous.

Be patient, shadowy woman:
Someday the ghastly destroyer
Who devours everyone
Will expunge my figure.

He'll come down to my yellowing books.
Rising on his toes, with cheeks
Lightly puffed, in the action

Of a regnant lord bored to death,
With one tired breath
He'll blow me to oblivion.

3. Solitude

I could fling my heart
from here to that roof:
my heart would whirl
and nobody see it.

I could shout out agonies
until my body cracked:
they would deliquesce
in the watery river.

I could dance
on the housetop a dance
of dark doom:
winds would kidnap
my dance.

I could,
uncaging the torch in my breast,
send it spinning
like witch's fire:
street lamps would
black it out.

4. Melancholy

Oh, death, I love you; but life, I adore you . . .
When I leave in a box, asleep forever,
Tell the spring sun to slip under
My eyelids one last time.

Leave me a moment beneath warm skies;
Let the fertile sun invade my ice . .
What a lovely star he was, rising
Each dawn, telling me: good morning.

I don't fear rest, to rest is only good.
But before my pilgrim grants his parting kiss,
How happy as a child, every
Morning, he always comes to my windows.

5. The Lie

I'm yours, God knows why, tomorrow at best
You'll drop me cold, and under my thralled
Eyes your lustful wish will be welded
With someone else's — but I choose being lost.

I'm sure someday I'll see this thing dead;
Already I watch for some sign of your whim,
Am offhand about rivals, even hum
Praise for a woman you've had.

You're really not as deep as you think.
You ramble on, con me with rank
Theatre and stereotyped scenes.

I listen and smile and seem bewitched,
And think: magnetic man, don't rush:
The better liar is my dream.

6. I Will Sleep

Flowers for teeth, dew for a cowl,
herbs as hands, dearest nurse,
smooth your earthy sheets for me
and a quilt of wool moss.

Nurse, I'll sleep, bed me down.
Put a lamp above my head,
a constellation; you choose one;
any one; dim it a little.

Leave: I hear the opening buds . . .
A seraph's foot rocks my cradle
and a bird drugs me by tracing compasses

on the sky. . . Thanks. Oh, yes,
if he telephones again tell him, won't you,
It's pointless, that I've just left. . . .

(written on the eve of her suicide)

Our July Is Rosy White

for Howard Jurgrau

> *"Answer July –*
> *Where is the Bee –*
> *Where is the Blush. . .?"*
>
> Emily Dickinson

Skiffs by the shore, it was truly picturesque —
the July rental you found in a village on the
    ocean's edge.
Yet you filled your last rolls only with
    photos
of mimosa blossoms.   No drifts of flotsam,
    no puffy sails,
just blooms close-up — surprising us later into
    silence.

The mimosa tree — was she your loving
    nurse,
petalling your window, shuttering you
from the blue summer sea, sending her
    afterglow
into your mortal room?
And you, thankful from every angle?

What truth lay blossom-hidden
at the end of the faraway sea —
where the dead of winter sprawls,
where Cape Horn looms black toward the
    Pole
in ice so southerly it can never fracture?

Our July is rosy white and lovely. At night
we read Emerson, he's pausing in his
    Concord
orchard as July blazes up — and the pear-
    studded branches
vanish! Now his bride Ellen, 19,
    long-gone, again sits
in the sunshine of his heart-shut house,
    writing.

We read more, are led into that other July,
at the Horn. Strung out by gales and sick,
Melville watches an honest Nantucketer,
Ray, 25, flying from the topmast — like
    the last chip
of flesh whipped off a long bone.

The warmth of our July betrayed us. You
     flew,
galed from the bone,   piercing all latitudes —
and the Horn waited, iced over by lights
     flashing pears
too far to gather into memory's lap,
no mimosa ever.

"This Is Verbena!"

for Cynthia

The moss accidentally
grew,
so well that the whole backyard
had the look of a billiard table.

My child and I, we
raked it gently. We expelled all grass. We'd
sweep one leaf off with our softest broom
toward a pocket by the fence.

We were soon Japanese about clutter,
about litter.
A praying mantis was barely permitted,
butterflies let in only if plain.

A botanist arrived, told us, "When moss
appears, it is a sign that soil lacks . . . ."

We would not hear what, would not
supply what.

My child and I, we
encouraged the moss,

praised the minimalism,
kept on narrowing the range of greens,

so that under our maple
never again would I cause
her eyes to darken
from pain and loss,

nor ever again
shake her small shoulders
in a hunger to hear her,
to arm her too soon
with my own armor,
the richness of syllables
then ripe in our garden —

"This is verbena!
This is gaillardia, this, portulaca,
this, hydrangea,
this, anemone" —

each flower
a poem
and a treachery.

Copper Beech

on the death of a colleague

Somewhere was where he went.

Now when the campus is thick with summer,
the copper beech
will show the small spaces

among its leaves
as clearly empty places.

And soon in winter
ever a larger

airy emptiness

will whirl
through the tines of its branches.

Then we'll turn our eyes away —
so hard it is to witness

the tree weeping twigs
as we lament.

A Vacation with My Grandson

for St. John

(i) The Jingle of Change

caught in his pocket —
five eagles — wings spread flat
on spinning moons

(ii) Nova Scotia Mist

mountains unscroll him
kayaking — paddle adagio —
forest tacet . . .

(iii) The Rosatis' Whippet

Old Woe — weary dog —
they've loved you eighteen summers —
the needle — so soon

(iv) Diane and St John and Young Woody

you two and one pup
in a green canoe — God sees
three peas in a pod

(v) Doctor Rosati Worries

asparagus sets —
deer-lopped — only onions for
his gourmet soup!

(vi) Maine Hiking Trail

ticks, bees, deerflies, gnats
and a thousand wooden snakes —
is this your Eden?

(vii) Canasta on Mt. Desert Island

shuffle the cards — cool!
the cabin is merry when we
drum up Las Vegas

(viii) Fourth Day

if you don't shower
now, I'll turn red-hot with rage
and break haiku rules

(ix) Sailing in a Storm

huge phantoms loom — growl —
leap! — from black horizon toward
shore-wishing crew — me

(x) At Home in Manhattan

miss rolling meadows?
I listen to rolling tires —
sweet rubbery rain

Rose Jones, Cleaning–Woman

Hospital switchboard operator:
"Mrs. Jones expired a half hour ago."

Now you are dead thirty minutes
I will dream you

in layers
of the rain's gray light

and the dream has you singing
elegant notes
thin as silver knives

with your arms leaning
like sleeping rabbits
against your window

as long wet mercuries roll down the pane
cracking it changeably

and dreaming you
I dust secret corners in your feelings
and dream loaves of mutual balm

and you, dreaming, fire me to sweeping
all the glum minerals out
of Bed–Stuy, out,
out to the edges of the rivers,

and your sister, kneeling, bangs
tin pans
to erase with crashes
the drunken man at your funeral,
with his steel eyes and lips,
and the thunder climbs
calling back a green Carolina universe

while under the shadows of our morning noises
you sing carvings

and make a church
of gray layers there
in your newest neatness.

Morning in Connecticut with My Grandson

The webby beauty of snow
trawling downhill
catches our January trees.

Think of Simon Peter's nets
slung around his prey
all pale with rapture.

We've turned our glassy tv off,
to a gray like the sky. We've
damped its terrorisms and cataclysms.

In white bowls,
glittering oatmeal,
sugared and buttered,
presence of form and aroma,
lamp of love!

My tall fourteener
sitting sleepy and simpático
in the kitchen rocker.

Few things go past
these uncurtained windows.
It's a stillness.

Yes, we've noted an automobile
that has just borne off
a pair of taillights, small red roses,
into the mist.

Yes, some minutes ago, we saw
a fountain of mashed ice
whorl up,
pushed by the brights on
a slow Mack truck.

As for us, we're absolute,
we're *here* in a morning,
tucking into breakfast
with mirthful hearts.

The Consolation in Being History

I. Winter

Then slowly turning unplayful, my mother's days
were nearly still,
becoming a frieze,

each abutting a long file of earlier days,
and paling more
the more recent.

In the last of the line of them,
she breathed such thin breathing
onto her merest memories —

of a red (the satin on a candybox lid),
a green (the lake lying under the trees),
a purple (the dusk fallen between her daughters) —

that they
bleached away
also.

II. Spring

Sister's door,
brother's door,
locked shut.

Mother's door,
father's door,
grass plots.

III. Autumn

With nowhere at all to place love,
I watched mummers
in a darkened barn on the straw hat circuit.

They were kind, were in a dumb show:
they looped themselves, braided air, caressed
a knee, lifted a wrist.

At the end, the music of flute stretched and
    collapsed

like a barber's strop,
and the footlights dimmed

to blue
and seemed the distant heaven
that is ever greedy for those we once have kissed.

IV. Winter

Wrapped in family silence,
I look at the February sea

until it seems the black marble of a tomb —
miles wide
and quarried long ago in the haze
of an Italian morning,
its rough planes surprised
by the stonecutter.

On the morning of our mother's baptism,
was it already in the making?

Who ordained it then, so black
and heavy, to ride,
an ocean on an ocean,

to this Atlantic beach,
to crash here and transmute,

becoming, as I look, a surface
of Mediterranean prisms
and Adriatic hushings?
Minnows of light, love's whispers —
one needs these.

V. Summer

My brother, of the U.S. Army, has come into town!
He'll buy us a fish lunch

at the Rose Café,
the fans will whirr sweetly over our heads,
preserving in song his chopper's rescues,

the waiter
will snap to,

and I will drink in the sunniness
of the daisies in their stark vase.

The Back Porch

(They say poets need "a deep prospect" for a view.)

you open
the screen door
and you step into the porch's night

I'm settled there
sipping an icy yellow drink

my glass
the glittering lighthouse
that saved my brother's toy ships
from evil waters

and the kitchen window
at my back
a dim illumination
in a medieval Book of Hours

the dark yard yes
lies perfect before me
the fence at its foot
dovetailing its side
and beyond
bushes in waves and cresting shrubs

and grand trees in silhouette
and foreign yards

deeper
a garden lamp drizzling light

it's true such depth
beckons one's thoughts
over long distances

yet you my daughter
have come to sit near me
ready for our soft talk

that never fails to engender
a surprise in my spirit

Primavera

for Cynthia, again

My child
curved over the sill
of the unmuzzled window,
saw morning air
shimmer on pins of grass.

Suddenly! she looped and arched
in summer-ish art. She plucked
a pair of roses,
thin cotton socks, from a pearwood box,
and into each rosey rose she
slipped a thin foot silkily.

For seersucker trousers then
she picked a pair
green and candesecent and
flimsily pitted as though
blown besotted from a brittle-pickle barrel
dizzily all ill-matched
with her blouse a blowing gauzy cage
dotted in blue-blotted
parakeet haunches.
And she yoked on

a yellow streamer,
wacky parabola her yellow ribbon!

Each tag of dress
a fetterless flag,
chalk zigzags,
unpartnered curves,
not, in the lot, an easy echo.
No harmonies inside
that springtime child.
She'd fragment all patterns . . .
she'd toot
an unknown and clarion jazz . . . .

An Italian Morning

Critical Reviews

"What a cornucopia Vinni Marie DAmbrosio offers with *An Italian Morning*! With wit and wisdom, this collection of poems and translations awakens the reader to the natural beauty and simple pleasures of existence. At the same time, it does not flinch from addressing the losses.

"D'Ambrosio's ample gifts embellish the work: her fine ear for nuances of language, her painterly eye that draws us to the visible world, as in 'The Blue-Ringed Tower in El Centro, CA' and the nature-drenched poems of New York ('Love Upstate') and Maine ('Maine, 1. Summer, pianissimo and '2. Winter, fortissimo'). There is healing, too, as in 'Aubade' to her former husband, a delight in family with poems to her daughter and grandson, and a humanistic reaching out to neglected figures such as 'Rose Jones,' the moving elegy for her cleaning woman. We find fresh appreciations of Shakespeare and the poetry in Herman Melville's *Moby-Dick*. We discover the command of craft that unpretentiously pervades the work. And as an understated yet no less significant bounty, we have D'Ambrosio's exquisite translations from Spanish that importantly draw attention to a brilliant and tragic figure, Alfonsina Storni (1892-1938).

"Wallace Stevens wrote that a poem 'refreshes life.' Indeed, D'Ambrosio's *An Italian Morning* achieves this triumph by appealing to heart, mind, and spirit."

—D.H. Melhem, poet, novelist, scholar, musical dramatist, six books of poems,
including *Conversations with a Stonemason, Country, Rest in Love*

"Whether evoking the primal marshes of Brooklyn, a pearwood box in a child's room, paradise regained with trombones and tropical flora, or 'The Consolation in Being History,' as well as her own romantic histories recreated with humor and subtle wit, Vinni Marie D'Ambrosio is a master of language with a musician's ear, a painter's eye, and a true *joie de vivre* – gifts to the world she loves."

—Roberta Gould, poet, nine books of poems, including *Not by Blood Alone, Houses with Ladders, Esta Naranja*

". . . [A] master of imagery . . . The lyrical sweep of D'Ambrosio's poems swirls you from individual flower petals to the white dust of winter in a feast of superb images. In *An Italian Morning* her emotional range is as wide as her imagistic spectrum."

—Karen Swenson, poet, five books of poems including *A Daughter's Latitude* and *The Lady from Bangkok*

". . . [P]rosodically carefree, the poems in Vinni Marie D'Ambrosio's new collection . . . display the author's sensual delight in language, a contagious linguistic playfulness that propels the willing reader to all manner of exotic and even ordinary but vividly detailed settings and memories."

—Martin Mitchell, editor-in-chief, *Rattapallax, Pivot, Athanor*

" *An Italian Morning* is a book of exquisite response to the recollection of natural and romantic wonder – and its unending power of sensuous grace.   D'Ambrosio's lyricism is enchanting . . . . Her poems sing of what is to be taken and given back in the experience of living."

—Prof. Martin Tucker, L.I.U., editor-in-chief *Confrontation, Library of Literary Criticism*, other literary critical series, and four books of poems

" . . . [B]rought to being simply and elegantly . . . The subject matter always a grand surprise and the telling equally magical, these poems glow without artifice."

—Ilsa Gilbert, poet, librettist, lyricist, *The Bundle Man, One Night Together*, and other chamber operas

"One of the most innovative ideas, one that brings out the layers of richness in her thinking, are the 'Interlude' pieces: the found poems and translations — the kind of audacity that flings us into other worlds. Absolutely riveting."

—Carol Wreszin, poet

"Many of D'Ambrosio's poems in *An Italian Morning* are playful and self-ironic, yet they affect us in an unexpectedly profound way. While her vision is optimistic in the face of the disappointments and tragedies that confront us, we "get" her seriousness. Over the years, as well, I've been impressed personally by her long and serious dedication to the art. She makes us believe that we all need poetry."

—Prof. Thelma Jurgrau, SUNY, scholar, translator, editor of George Sand's *Autobiography*

A graduate of Smith College and New York University, Vinni Marie D'Ambrosio, Ph. D., lives in New York City. She is a poet and scholar whose work is found in anthologies, journals, newspapers, as well as in her collection of poems, *Life of Touching Mouths* (New York University Press), in her long narrative poem, *Mexican Gothic* (about Frida Kahlo and Diego Rivera, woodcuts by Karen Kunc, Blue Heron Press), and in her cultural study of T.S. Eliot's youth, *Eliot Possessed* (New York University Press). Her poem "Copper Beech" appears on a public memorial monument commissioned by New York City. Her work has also been published in Thailand and Italy. D'Ambrosio has given readings all over the United States and in Canada. Her awards have included poet-in-residence at San Diego State University and two fellowships from the Virginia Center for the Creative Arts, as well as dozens of prizes for her poems. For twelve years she was the director of poetry readings at the Brooklyn Museum. She was also president of the T.S. Eliot Society in St. Louis and the Pen & Brush, Inc., in New York City. Professor Emerita of Brooklyn College of the City University of New York, D'Ambrosio currently leads an ongoing seminar in the poetry classics at the American Association of University Women, New York City Branch.

An Italian Morning

Poems
by
Vinni Marie D'Ambrosio